Co

CW00662536

General Knowledge

1) Bolton's first game of the 21st century was a 2-0 home loss to which team on the 3rd of January 2000?

2) Which company replaced Reebok as the club's main shirt sponsor ahead of the 2009/10 season?

3) Which player was the clubs top scorer in the 2012/13 Championship season?

4) How many points were Bolton deducted in the 2019/20 League One season for entering administration?

5) Who became the first Croatian to appear for the club after signing in 2009?

6) Which team did Bolton beat 5-2 on aggregate in the First Division Play-Off Semi Final in 2001?

7) How many games did Bolton win during the 2015/16 Championship season which led to their relegation to League One?

8) Who became the youngest ever player to represent Bolton when he debuted against Coventry City in August 2019?

9) Bolton missed out on a place in the Championship Play-Offs in 2013 after failing to beat which side on the last day of the season?

10) Which goalkeeper played against West Brom aged 41 in January 2005?

11) What shirt number did Joey O'Brien wear throughout his time at the club?

12) Jay Jay Okocha replaced who as the club captain in 2003?

13) Johan Elmander scored with a solo effort by producing a stunning turn in a tight space then slotting home against which club in November 2010?

14) Which Bolton player scored an own goal in the 2-0 home loss to Blackburn in November 2009?

15) Jussi Jaaskelainen saved two penalties in the 1-0 victory over which side in October 2006?

16) Fredi Bobic scored a Premiership hat-trick against which side in April 2002?

17) Who retired in 2012 having made over 400 appearances for Bolton?

18) Ivan Campo scored from almost 40 yards out with a stunning effort against which team in August 2006?

19) Bolton gained automatic promotion from League Two by finishing in what position in the 2020/21 season?

20) Bolton avoided relegation on the last day of the 2002/03 Premiership season by beating which team 2-1?

Transfers 2000-2010

1) Which striker was sold to Chelsea in June 2000?

2) From which club did Bolton buy Michael Ricketts in the summer of 2000?

3) Which central defender arrived from Coventry City in February 2001?

4) Which defender left to join Newcastle in the summer of 2001?

5) From which club did Bolton sign Youri Djorkaeff on a free transfer in 2002?

6) Who was signed from Olympiakos in May 2003?

7) Which club was Michael Ricketts sold to in the 2003 January transfer window?

8) Bolton bought who from Sporting Lisbon in August 2003?

9) From which club did Les Ferdinand join in 2004?

10) Who did Emerson Thome sign for after leaving the club in 2004?

11) Which Mexican joined Bolton from Pachuca in 2005?

12) Which centre back joined Birmingham City on a free transfer from Bolton in August 2006?

13) Bolton brought in which two players from Aston Villa in the summer of 2007?

14) From which club did Bolton purchase Matty Taylor in 2008?

15) Which forward was bought from Toulouse in June 2008?

16) Bolton sold which striker to Chelsea in January 2008?

17) Which central defender was bought from Watford in August 2008?

18) Who did Ivan Campo sign for after leaving Bolton in 2008?

19) From which team was Sam Ricketts signed in 2009?

20) Which player did Bolton sign from Real Madrid in the summer of 2010?

Cup Games

1) Who scored a hat-trick in the 5-2 win over Walsall in the FA Cup Third Round in 2019?

2) Bolton beat Lokomotiv Plovdiv in the UEFA Cup First Round in 2005 by what aggregate score-line?

3) Marseille knocked Bolton out of the UEFA Cup in February 2006, but which Bolton player had put them ahead in the tie by opening the scoring in the second leg?

4) Bolton reached the Quarter-Final of the League Cup in 2001 but then slumped to defeat against Spurs by what score?

5) Which team knocked Bolton out of the EFL Trophy in the Second Round in 2019?

6) Bolton reached the FA Cup Semi-Final in 2011 by beating Birmingham City 3-2 with a last minute winner from who?

7) What was the final score in the devastating loss to Stoke City in that subsequent Semi-Final?

8) Aston Villa were beaten by Bolton by what aggregated score in the 2004 League Cup Semi-Final?

9) Who scored the only goal as Bolton knocked Atletico Madrid out of the UEFA Cup in 2008?

10) Which team knocked Bolton out of the 2007/08 UEFA Cup?

11) Bolton beat Arsenal 1-0 in the FA Cup Fourth Round in 2006 with a goal from who?

Memorable Games

1) Who scored a brace in the 4-3 away win over Blackburn in January 2004?

2) Who opened the scoring in the dramatic 3-2 victory over Nottingham Forest on the final day of the 2017/18 Championship season?

3) By what score-line did Bolton hammer Stoke in November 2011?

4) Bolton claimed a 5-0 away win over which team on the opening day of the 2001/02 Premiership season?

5) Leeds United were smashed by what score at Elland Road in March 2014?

6) Bolton fought back from 2-0 down with just over 10 minutes remaining to claim a 3-2 away win at which side in League Two in February 2021?

7) Who scored the late winner to beat Arsenal 2-1 at home in the Premier League in April 2011?

8) Leeds United were smashed by what score at Elland Road in March 2014?

9) Who scored two penalties during the 5-1 win over Newcastle in November 2010?

10) Who scored the only goal in the derby win over Blackburn in December 2015?

11) What was the final score in the victory over Ipswich at Portman Road in League One in September 2021?

Red Cards

1) Bolton hung on for a 0-0 draw away to Blackburn in January 2006 after which player was dismissed in the first half?

2) Which two players were sent off as nine-man Bolton collapsed from 2-0 up to lose 3-2 at Charlton in 2013?

3) Mark Little was dismissed in the match against which team in February 2018?

4) Which on-loan player was sent off against Manchester City in May 2011?

5) Jason Lowe was shown a red card during the 1-1 draw with which team in December 2019?

6) Jlloyd Samuel was sent off for a professional foul against which opposition in October 2009?

7) Who was dismissed inside the first 20 minutes of the 2-0 home defeat against Everton in November 2011?

8) Marc Wilson was sent off in a 0-0 draw with which team in September 2018?

9) Which two Wanderers players saw red in the fiery encounter with Leicester City which ended 2-2 in December 2001?

10) Who was sent off eleven minutes into his debut against Morecambe in February 2021?

Managers

1) Who was the manager of Bolton Wanderers at the beginning of the 21st century?

2) Who took over as manager when Sam Allardyce left the club in 2007?

3) Which team did Gary Megson face in his face game as boss?

4) Which team did Owen Coyle leave to take up the job at Bolton?

5) Bolton lost 4-0 to which club in Dougie Freedman's last game in charge?

6) Which coach was given the job as caretaker manager on three occasions this century?

7) Who was manager as the club were promoted from League One in 2017?

8) Bolton beat Blackburn 4-0 in March 2014 under the leadership of which manager?

9) How many league wins did Keith Hill achieve as Bolton manager in the 31 League One matches he took charge of?

10) Ian Evatt gained his first win as boss in an away match against which team in October 2020?

First Goals

Can you name the club that these players scored their first goal for the club against?

1) Youri Djorkaeff
a) Charlton Athletic
b) Blackburn Rovers
c) Newcastle United

2) Ivan Campo
a) Manchester City
b) Arsenal
c) Liverpool

3) Kevin Davies
a) Southampton
b) Chelsea
c) Blackburn Rovers

4) Chris Basham
a) Chelsea
b) Sheffield United
c) Newcastle United

5) Daniel Sturridge
a) **Wolves**
b) **Newcastle United**
c) **Manchester City**

6) Mark Davies
a) **Bradford City**
b) **Leyton Orient**
c) **Tranmere Rovers**

7) Jermaine Beckford
a) **Tranmere Rovers**
b) **Portsmouth**
c) **Sunderland**

8) Sammy Ameobi
a) **Birmingham City**
b) **Blackpool**
c) **Nottingham Forest**

9) Aaron Wilbraham
a) **Sheffield Wednesday**
b) **Nottingham Forest**
c) **Birmingham City**

10) Antoni Sarcevic

a) **Bradford City**
b) **Southend**
c) **Sunderland**

Transfers 2011-2021

1) Which defender arrived from Middlesbrough in January 2011?

2) Bolton signed which two players from Burnley in July 2011?

3) Goalkeeper Jussi Jaaskelainen joined which team in June 2012?

4) From which team did Keith Andrews sign on a free in 2012?

5) Which Spanish club did Martin Petrov join in January 2013?

6) Which midfielder moved to Bolton from Liverpool in August 2013?

7) Who did David N'Gog move to after leaving Bolton?

8) Which player returned to Bolton from Cub Brugge in December 2014?

9) From which Australian team was Emile Heskey signed in 2014?

10) Goalkeeper Adam Bogdan joined which Premier League side in 2015?

11) Which experienced striker signed from Crystal Palace in October 2015?

12) From which club was Adam Le Fondre signed in 2017?

13) Which defender was sold to Arsenal in July 2016?

14) From which club did Bolton bring in Aaron Wilbraham in 2017?

15) Which forward move to Bolton on a free transfer from Sheffield United in July 2018?

16) From where was Jacob Mellis signed in January 2020?

17) Remi Matthews decided to join which League One side in August 2020?

18) Bolton brought in which player from Feyenoord in June 2021?

19) Which player made a loan move to Bolton from Hamburg in July 2021?

20) From which club did Elias Kachunga arrive in the summer of 2021?

Answers

General Knowledge Answers

1) Bolton's first game of the 21st century was a 2-0 home loss to which team on the 3rd of January 2000?
Walsall

2) Which company replaced Reebok as the club's main shirt sponsor ahead of the 2009/10 season?
188Bet

3) Which player was the clubs top scorer in the 2012/13 Championship season?
Chris Eagles

4) How many points were Bolton deducted in the 2019/20 League One season for entering administration?
12

5) Who became the first Croatian to appear for the club after signing in 2009?
Ivan Klasnic

6) Which team did Bolton beat 5-2 on aggregate in the First Division Play-Off Semi Final in 2001?
West Brom

7) How many games did Bolton win during the 2015/16 Championship season which led to their relegation to League One?
Five

8) Who became the youngest ever player to represent Bolton when he debuted against Coventry City in August 2019?
Finlay Lockett

9) Bolton missed out on a place in the Championship Play-Offs in 2013 after failing to beat which side on the last day of the season?
Blackpool

10) Which goalkeeper played against West Brom aged 41 in January 2005?
Kevin Poole

11) What shirt number did Joey O'Brien wear throughout his time at the club?

24

12) Jay Jay Okocha replaced who as the club captain in 2003?

Gudni Bergsson

13) Johan Elmander scored with a solo effort by producing a stunning turn in a tight space then slotting home against which club in November 2010?

Wolverhampton Wanderers

14) Which Bolton player scored an own goal in the 2-0 home loss to Blackburn in November 2009?

Sam Ricketts

15) Jussi Jaaskelainen saved two penalties in the 1-0 victory over which side in October 2006?

Blackburn Rovers

16) Fredi Bobic scored a Premiership hat-trick against which side in April 2002?
Ipswich Town

17) Who retired in 2012 having made over 400 appearances for Bolton?
Ricardo Gardner

18) Ivan Campo scored from almost 40 yards out with a stunning effort against which team in August 2006?
Tottenham Hotspur

19) Bolton gained automatic promotion from League Two by finishing in what position in the 2020/21 season?
Third

20) Bolton avoided relegation on the last day of the 2002/03 Premiership season by beating which team 2-1?
Middlesbrough

Transfers 2000-2010 Answers

1) Which striker was sold to Chelsea in
   June 2000?
   Eidur Gudjohnsen

2) From which club did Bolton buy Michael
   Ricketts in the summer of 2000?
   Walsall

3) Which central defender arrived from
   Coventry City in February 2001?
   Colin Hendry

4) Which defender left to join Newcastle in
   the summer of 2001?
   Robbie Elliott

5) From which club did Bolton sign Youri
   Djorkaeff on a free transfer in 2002?
   Kaiserslautern

6) Who was signed from Olympiakos in
   May 2003?
   Stelios Giannakopoulos

7) Which club was Michael Ricketts sold to in the 2003 January transfer window?
Middlesbrough

8) Bolton bought who from Sporting Lisbon in August 2003?
Mario Jardel

9) From which club did Les Ferdinand join in 2004?
Leicester City

10) Who did Emerson Thome sign for after leaving the club in 2004?
Wigan Athletic

11) Which Mexican joined Bolton from Pachuca in 2005?
Jared Borgetti

12) Which centre back joined Birmingham City on a free transfer from Bolton in August 2006?
Radhi Jaidi

13) Bolton brought in which two players from Aston Villa in the summer of 2007?
Jlloyd Samuel and Gavin McCann

14) From which club did Bolton purchase Matty Taylor in 2008?
Portsmouth

15) Which forward was bought from Toulouse in June 2008?
Johan Elmander

16) Bolton sold which striker to Chelsea in January 2008?
Nicolas Anelka

17) Which central defender was bought from Watford in August 2008?
Danny Shittu

18) Who did Ivan Campo sign for after leaving Bolton in 2008?
Ipswich Town

19) From which team was Sam Ricketts signed in 2009?
Hull City

20) Which player did Bolton sign from Real Madrid in the summer of 2010?
Marcos Alonso

Cup Games Answers

1) Who scored a hat-trick in the 5-2 win over Walsall in the FA Cup Third Round in 2019?
Josh Magennis

2) Bolton beat Lokomotiv Plovdiv in the UEFA Cup First Round in 2005 by what aggregate score-line?
4-2

3) Marseille knocked Bolton out of the UEFA Cup in February 2006, but which Bolton player had put them ahead in the tie by opening the scoring in the second leg?
Stelios Giannakopoulos

4) Bolton reached the Quarter-Final of the League Cup in 2001 but then slumped to defeat against Spurs by what score?
Tottenham 6-0 Bolton

5) Which team knocked Bolton out of the EFL Trophy in the Second Round in 2019?
Accrington Stanley

6) Bolton reached the FA Cup Semi-Final in 2011 by beating Birmingham City 3-2 with a last minute winner from who?
Chung-yong Lee

7) What was the final score in the devastating loss to Stoke City in that subsequent Semi-Final?
Bolton 0-5 Stoke City

8) Aston Villa were beaten by Bolton by what aggregated score in the 2004 League Cup Semi-Final?
Bolton 5-4 Aston Villa

9) Who scored the only goal as Bolton knocked Atletico Madrid out of the UEFA Cup in 2008?
El-Hadji Diouf

10) Which team knocked Bolton out of the 2007/08 UEFA Cup?
Sporting Lisbon

11) Bolton beat Arsenal 1-0 in the FA Cup Fourth Round in 2006 with a goal from who?
Stelios Giannakopoulos

Memorable Games Answers

1) Who scored a brace in the 4-3 away win over Blackburn in January 2004?
Kevin Nolan

2) Who opened the scoring in the dramatic 3-2 victory over Nottingham Forest on the final day of the 2017/18 Championship season?
Adam Le Fondre

3) By what score-line did Bolton hammer Stoke in November 2011?
Bolton 5-0 Stoke

4) Bolton claimed a 5-0 away win over which team on the opening day of the 2001/02 Premiership season?
Leicester City

5) Leeds United were smashed by what score at Elland Road in March 2014?
Leeds 1-5 Bolton

6) Bolton fought back from 2-0 down with just over 10 minutes remaining to claim a 3-2 away win at which side in League Two in February 2021?
Mansfield

7) Who scored the late winner to beat Arsenal 2-1 at home in the Premier League in April 2011?
Tamir Cohen

8) Leeds United were smashed by what score at Elland Road in March 2014?
Leeds 1-5 Bolton

9) Who scored two penalties during the 5-1 win over Newcastle in November 2010?
Kevin Davies

10) Who scored the only goal in the derby win over Blackburn in December 2015?
Gary Madine

11) What was the final score in the victory over Ipswich at Portman Road in League One in September 2021?
Ipswich 2-5 Bolton

Red Cards Answers

1) Bolton hung on for a 0-0 draw away to Blackburn in January 2006 after which player was dismissed in the first half?
Hidetoshi Nakata

2) Which two players were sent off as nine-man Bolton collapsed from 2-0 up to lose 3-2 at Charlton in 2013?
Sam Ricketts and Craig Davies

3) Mark Little was dismissed in the match against which team in February 2018?
QPR

4) Which on-loan player was sent off against Manchester City in May 2011?
Daniel Sturridge

5) Jason Lowe was shown a red card during the 1-1 draw with which team in December 2019?
Shrewsbury

6) Jlloyd Samuel was sent off for a professional foul against which opposition in October 2009?
Chelsea

7) Who was dismissed inside the first 20 minutes of the 2-0 home defeat against Everton in November 2011?
David Wheater

8) Marc Wilson was sent off in a 0-0 draw with which team in September 2018?
Ipswich Town

9) Which two Wanderers players saw red in the fiery encounter with Leicester City which ended 2-2 in December 2001?
Paul Warhurst and Dean Holdsworth

10) Who was sent off eleven minutes into his debut against Morecambe in February 2021?
Marcus Maddison

Managers Answers

1) Who was the manager of Bolton Wanderers at the beginning of the 21st century?
Sam Allardyce

2) Who took over as manager when Sam Allardyce left the club in 2007?
Sammy Lee

3) Which team did Gary Megson face in his face game as boss?
Braga

4) Which team did Owen Coyle leave to take up the job at Bolton?
Burnley

5) Bolton lost 4-0 to which club in Dougie Freedman's last game in charge?
Fulham

6) Which coach was given the job as caretaker manager on three occasions this century?
Jimmy Phillips

7) Who was manager as the club were promoted from League One in 2017?
Phil Parkinson

8) Bolton beat Blackburn 4-0 in March 2014 under the leadership of which manager?
Dougie Freedman

9) How many league wins did Keith Hill achieve as Bolton manager in the 31 League One matches he took charge of?
Five

10) Ian Evatt gained his first win as boss in an away match against which team in October 2020?
Harrogate Town

First Goals Answers

1) Youri Djorkaeff
   Charlton Athletic

2) Ivan Campo
   Liverpool

3) Kevin Davies
   Blackburn Rovers

4) Chris Basham
   Chelsea

5) Daniel Sturridge
   Wolves

6) Mark Davies
   Tranmere Rovers

7) Jermaine Beckford
   Tranmere Rovers

8) Sammy Ameobi
   Blackpool

9) Aaron Wilbraham
   Sheffield Wednesday

10) Antoni Sarcevic
    Bradford City

Transfers 2011-2021 Answers

1) Which defender arrived from Middlesbrough in January 2011?
   David Wheater

2) Bolton signed which two players from Burnley in July 2011?
   Chris Eagles and Tyrone Mears

3) Goalkeeper Jussi Jaaskelainen joined which team in June 2012?
   West Ham

4) From which team did Keith Andrews sign on a free in 2012?
   West Brom

5) Which Spanish club did Martin Petrov join in January 2013?
   Espanyol

6) Which midfielder moved to Bolton from Liverpool in August 2013?
   Jay Spearing

7) Who did David N'Gog move to after leaving Bolton?
Swansea City

8) Which player returned to Bolton from Cub Brugge in December 2014?
Eidur Gudjohnsen

9) From which Australian team was Emile Heskey signed in 2014?
Newcastle Jets

10) Goalkeeper Adam Bogdan joined which Premier League side in 2015?
Liverpool

11) Which experienced striker signed from Crystal Palace in October 2015?
Shola Ameobi

12) From which club was Adam Le Fondre signed in 2017?
Cardiff City

13) Which defender was sold to Arsenal in July 2016?
Rob Holding

14) From which club did Bolton bring in Aaron Wilbraham in 2017?
Bristol City

15) Which forward move to Bolton on a free transfer from Sheffield United in July 2018?
Clayton Donaldson

16) From where was Jacob Mellis signed in January 2020?
Mansfield

17) Remi Matthews decided to join which League One side in August 2020?
Sunderland

18) Bolton brought in which player from Feyenoord in June 2021?
George Johnston

19) Which player made a loan move to Bolton from Hamburg in July 2021?
Xavier Amaechi

20) From which club did Elias Kachunga arrive in the summer of 2021?
Sheffield Wednesday

*If you enjoyed this book please consider
leaving a five star review on Amazon*

Books by Jack Pearson available on Amazon:

Cricket:

Cricket World Cup 2019 Quiz Book
The Ashes 2019 Cricket Quiz Book
The Ashes 2010-2019 Quiz Book
The Ashes 2005 Quiz Book
The Indian Premier League Quiz Book

Football:

The Quiz Book of Premier League Football Transfers
The Quiz Book of the England Football Team in the 21st Century
The Quiz Book of Arsenal Football Club in the 21st Century
The Quiz Book of Aston Villa Football Club in the 21st Century
The Quiz Book of Chelsea Football Club in the 21st Century
The Quiz Book of Everton Football Club in the 21st Century

The Quiz Book of Leeds United Football Club in the 21st Century

The Quiz Book of Leicester City Football Club in the 21st Century

The Quiz Book of Liverpool Football Club in the 21st Century

The Quiz Book of Manchester City Football Club in the 21st Century

The Quiz Book of Manchester United Football Club in the 21st Century

The Quiz Book of Newcastle United Football Club in the 21st Century

The Quiz Book of Southampton Football Club in the 21st Century

The Quiz Book of Sunderland Association Football Club in the 21st Century

The Quiz Book of Tottenham Hotspur Football Club in the 21st Century

The Quiz Book of West Ham United Football Club in the 21st Century

The Quiz Book of Wrexham Association Football Club in the 21st Century

Printed in Great Britain
by Amazon